Re-Mind Yourself

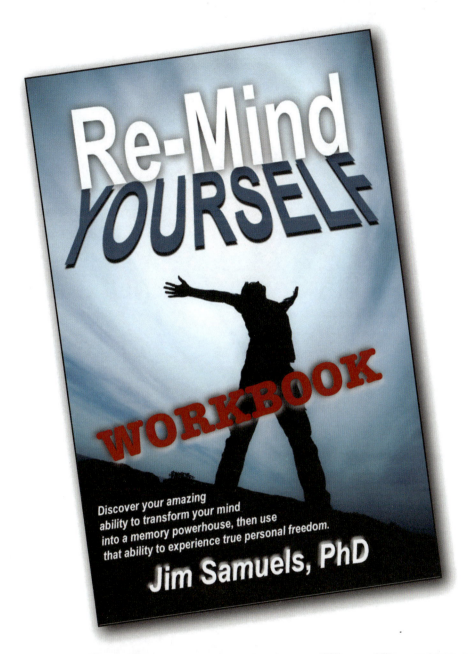

WORKBOOK

© 2012 by Dr. Jim Samuels, LLC

Re-Mind Yourself WORKBOOK

Jim Samuels, PhD

CreateSpace
U.S.A.

Re-Mind Yourself
Introductory Training for Re-Minding™
by
Jim Samuels, PhD

Samuels Institute of Memory Sciences 501 (c)(3)
a non-profit educational institution
PO Box 1321
Laguna Beach, CA 92652

No part of this course manual may be reproduced or transmitted in any form or by any means, electronic or mechanical, including photocopying, recording, or by any information storage and retrieval system, without permission in writing from the author, except for the inclusion for brief quotations in a review.

Copyright © 2012 by Jim Samuels, PhD
All rights reserved

Samuels, Jim
Re-Mind Yourself

ISBN-13: 978-1470046019
ISBN-10: 1470046016

Printed in the United States of America

Part I
Train Your Brain

Mnemonics (memory training) has been around and serving humanity for thousands of years.

You have an amazing memory. It just needs a little training for it to perform like never before. This is that training.

History of Re-Minding™

Re-Minding came out of an accidental application of mnemonics
I was driving my car and feeling overwhelmed by all the tasks I needed to accomplish. Instead of parking and writing a To-Do list, I memorized one. The sensation of stress relief and increased clarity was surprising. I then shared the idea with others by taking them through memorizing their own To-Do lists. They also felt relief and liked having their To-Do lists available all the time.

Eventually, thoughts and feelings that were worrisome were addressed in a similar way and Re-Minding was born.

The Shopping List

This is your practice shopping list

1- Mouth Wash
2- Tissues
3- Dog Food
4- Paper Towels
5- Tea
6- Newspaper
7- Milk
8- Bread
9- Cottage Cheese
10- Laundry Soap
11- Bottled Water
12- New pen

Take 90 seconds or so to try to memorize it by number.

Don't be concerned if this seems difficult. Most people have difficulty holding onto more than six items in short-term memory.

An untrained memory has the <u>ability</u>, but not the <u>skill</u> of remembering.

Before Training Test

Write the list here, from memory

1. _____
2. _____
3. _____
4. _____
5. _____
6. _____
7. _____
8. _____
9. _____
10. _____
11. _____
12. _____

Score ____/12

This is simply a starting point. <u>With a trained memory</u> this list could easily be 100 items long and you could expect to score in the high 90's.

Train Your Brain

Reminders

To gain control of your perceptions and reactions, you must first learn to harness your memory with reminders.

We'll start by giving you a numbered list that is easy to remember. This is a list of reminders that are designed to replace the numbers 1 through 12.

A New List of 12 Items

Training your memory for the first time will require a little patience until you discover how the process works best for you. For now, simply follow along, imagining the reminders shown. Don't work at it. Just look at them and notice that they look like their numbers.

This list is easier

To make these reminders easy to remember, each one is based on the shape of its number. Look at these first three.

Once you have learned these reminders you'll be using them the rest of your life. So, take your time learning them.

The Rest of The Reminders

Your Reminders

Write the list of reminders here, from memory

1. _____
2. _____
3. _____
4. _____
5. _____
6. _____
7. _____
8. _____
9. _____
10. _____
11. _____
12. _____

Score _____/12

Notice how much easier it is to remember this list? That's because the numbers themselves are used to remind you of the listed items.

We'll use this principle to memorize your shopping list.

3 Steps to Re-Minding

1 - **Clarify**

When memorizing a numbered list, always start by getting each number ready before clarifying what the item for that number is. For example, we'll start with number 1, so create an image of your candle in your imagination.

2 - **Capture**

We won't use number 1, instead, we'll use the candle. Since the number 1 item on our shopping list is mouthwash, we'll need to make a reminder that combines our candle with mouthwash. Put them together to capture that mouthwash at number one.

3 - **Convert**

Convert the idea of candle and mouthwash into a memorable reminder! Pour the mouthwash over your lit candle! Hear the hiss of the flame going out and make a "minty" mess!

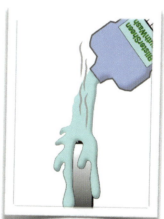

Actually imagine you are doing it! Experiences are much more memorable than mere words or pictures. By imagining yourself actually doing this with the candle and the mouthwash, it will make it much easier to recall later on.

Item 2 - Tissues

Next is number 2, so get your swan ready.

Number 2 on our list is a box of tissues.

We need to associate this to number 2, but we'll use a swan

Now we'll combine the tissues with the swan in a very memorable way...
Have your swan swallow the box of tissues!

Item 3 - Dog Food

Next is number 3 so get your glasses ready.

Number 3 on our shopping list is dog food, so we'll need to combine glasses with dog food.

Put some over-sized glasses on that dog!

Item 4 - Paper Towels

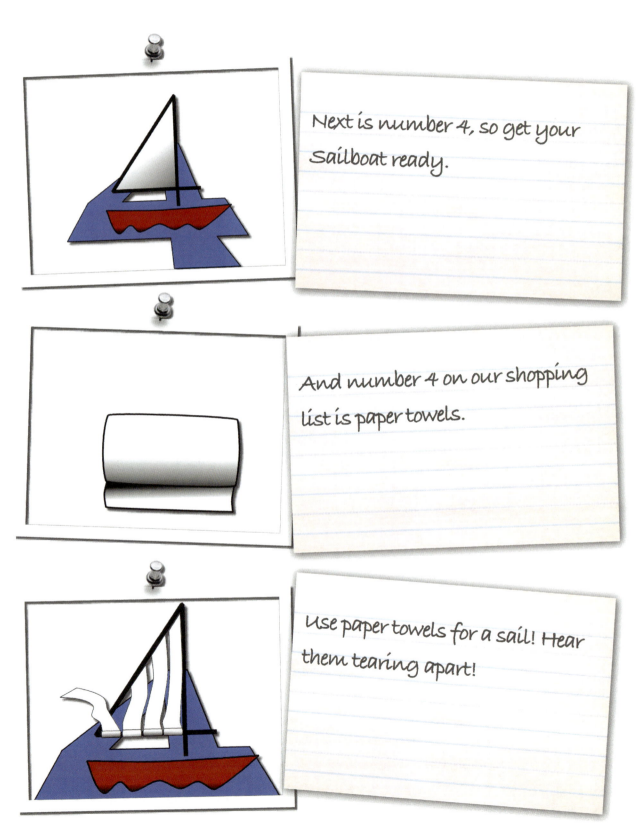

Item 5 - Tea

Next is number 5, so get your Star ready.

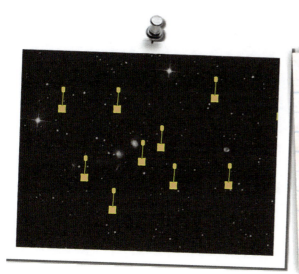

Imagine looking up into the night sky and seeing tea bags instead of stars!

Item 6 - Newspaper

Now, let me ask you something. If you were shopping and an actual elephant came up to you and handed you a newspaper, would you ever forget that?

Item 7 - Milk

Next is number 7 so get your Flag on a pole ready.

Number 7 on our shopping list is milk, so we'll need to combine a flag with a carton of milk.

Let's combine our flag with that milk carton by planting our flag in it and making a mess!

Item 8 - Loaf of Bread

8 is an hourglass, so get yours ready.

We need to combine our hourglass with a loaf of bread.

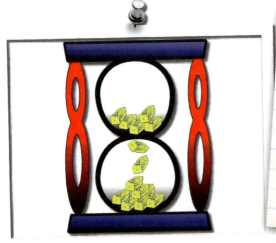

So, we'll look closely at our hourglass and see tiny little loaves of bread falling through it instead of sand!

Item 9 - Cottage Cheese

Get your cat ready for number nine.

Number 9 is cottage cheese, so have fun!

Item 10 - Laundry Soap

Imagine that you are at a baseball game. And the pitcher, instead of throwing a ball, throws a box of laundry soap! The batter swings, hits the soap, and it explodes all over the infield! It's a home run!

Item 11 - Bottled Water

Number 11 is a moneybag, so we'll need to create a reminder for our moneybag and bottled water. Hold up your moneybag, but have water running out of it, leaking all over you!

Item 12 - A New Pen

After Training Test

Write the shopping list here, from memory

1. _____
2. _____
3. _____
4. _____
5. _____
6. _____
7. _____
8. _____
9. _____
10. _____
11. _____
12. _____

Score _____/12

<u>With a trained memory</u> any numbered list of 12 items can easily and quickly be memorized and you can expect to score in the high 90's after reading or hearing it just once.

Tame Your Brain

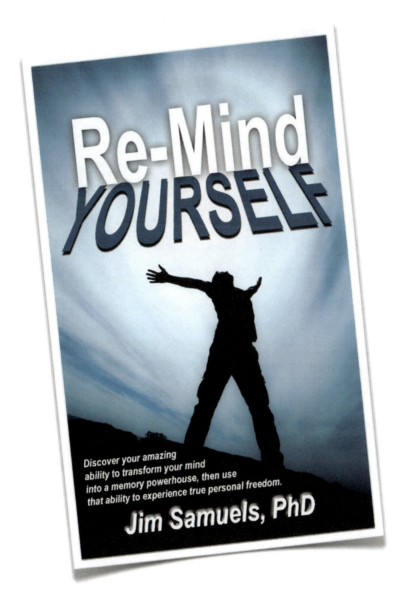

Now that you have some control over your memory, it's time to discover how powerful that control can be when it comes to taming unwanted, unpleasant thoughts and feelings.

Welcome to Re-Minding™

Joe's Re-Minding Session

Clarify, Capture, Convert.

You may remember our friend Joe from the Re-Mind Yourself course manual, who as a child was badly bitten, which resulted in a lifelong fear of dogs.

Clarify

First we had Joe focus on his unwanted feeling, in this case fear of dogs, and rate that fear on the -10 to +10 scale to further **clarify** and to engage his brain's analytical left hemisphere. At this point, his emotional and analytical processes were in agreement.

Capture

Second we had him capture the image of that dog in his imagination. Although the attack happened years ago, and he's been afraid of all dogs since the attack, it's really the dog that attacked him that "anchors" the fear in his mind.

Convert

Finally, we had Joe convert this image into a re-minder using the number 1 (a candle). This moved Joe from being the <u>effect</u> of the memory to being the <u>cause</u> of the memory. And, being the cause is a much more powerful position.

When Joe rated how he felt about the event again, it was up to a plus nine. He's felt that way ever since, and due to this change in his <u>perception memory</u>, he sees dogs differently now.

Perception memory is accessed at a rate of between 100 and 300 times per second, and is a pre-cognitive function of the brain, where your sensory input is compared to memory of prior perceptions so you can recognize what you are experiencing. More about this is covered in the Re-Mind Yourself manual.

This resulted in Joe laughing as he experienced a releasing of years of acquired stress on the subject of dogs. On our -10 to +10 scale, Joe went from a -9 to a +10. That's 19 points on a 20-point scale, or <u>a 95% improvement in the way he felt.</u>

Memory Power

We created a mnemonic memory for this event because mnemonic (trained) memories are significantly more powerful than "natural" memories. This new memory is strong enough to become the "primary" association in Joe's perception memory, and as such it triggers his primary perception and reaction when near a dog.

Lasting effects

The long term effects of successfully creating a re-minder are stable. Although Re-Minding has only been available since 2005, students report stable and continued results from the re-minders they created.

Your Journal

Your journal can be very helpful in several ways:

- Have an easy way to review your progress.
- Re-visit issues that need more work.
- Add up how much stress you have released.
- Notice how often you've been doing your sessions.
- Revitalize re-minders you've already made.
- Strengthen your motivation on your goals.
- Decide on new areas of your life to create more freedom for.
- Notice how much faster you are making your re-minders.

The Format

This is the format I suggest for each of your Re-Minding sessions.

(Your initials) Date and Time

Issue:
Rating:
Re-Minder:
New rating:

(If you do more than one re-minder, add the start time of each one.)
Time:
Issue:
Rating:
Re-Minder:
New rating:

Time:
Issue:
Rating:
Re-Minder:
New rating:

Time: (The time you complete your Re-Minding session.)

Duration (Total time for this session.)
Points (Total of ratings improvement.)
Points per minute (Divide the total points gained by minutes.)

My Hit List

This is the Re-Minding To-Do List

Any time you notice anything "gets to you," make certain you put it on this list. This is especially useful when you realize you have "pet peeves," annoyances or vulnerabilities to your peace of mind.

When you are doing regular Re-Minding sessions, you'll find there are times when the answer to the question, "Is anything bothering you?" is "No." A very nice place to be. When that happens, if you still want something to work on, turn to your Hit List in your journal and pick something you know would be nice to be free from.

The Plateaus of Potential

Some of the areas of your life that contain great potential are:

Body

Identity

Sex life

Family (parents, siblings, mate(s), kids)

Friends

Career, work life

Associates

Community, groups

Politics

Humanity

Pets, plants, other living things

Possessions

Energy

Time

Wealth

Education

Creativity

Spirit, spirituality

Infinity, god

Question: "Is anything bothering you about your (_____)?"

My Wish List

Improvements and Enjoyment

"Is there anything you would like to improve or enjoy more?"

This can be a wonderful question for exploring and expanding your personal experience of your life. Noticing the small improvements you can make, along with taking the time to actually enjoy what you are experiencing, is a real life-changer.

This is where you work on your "freedom to".

Use the same Plateaus of Potential to build up a "Wish List" of increased awareness and freedom.

"Is there anything you would like to improve or enjoy more about your (_____)?"

Body
Identity
Sex life
Family (parents, siblings, mate(s), kids)
Friends
Career, work life
Associates
Community, groups
Politics
Humanity
Pets, plants, other living things
Possessions
Energy
Time
Wealth
Education
Creativity
Spirit, spirituality
Infinity, god

My Hit List

Item	Date	Rate	Re-Minder	Rate

Item	Date	Rate	Re-Minder	Rate

Item	Date	Rate	Re-Minder	Rate

Item	Date	Rate	Re-Minder	Rate

Item	Date	Rate	Re-Minder	Rate

My Wish List

Item	Date	Rate	Re-Minder	Rate

Item	Date	Rate	Re-Minder	Rate

Item	Date	Rate	Re-Minder	Rate

Item	Date	Rate	Re-Minder	Rate

Courses

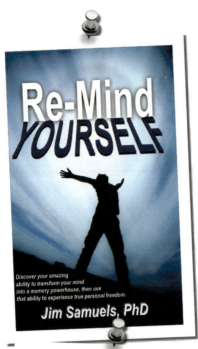

RE-MIND YOURSELF
Jim Samuels, Ph.D.
ISBN-13: 978-1468098129
ISBN-10: 1468098128

This is the course manual that this workbook is the companion to. It can be very helpful to use the course manual when working your way through this workbook.

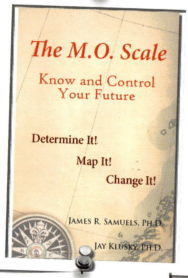

THE M.O. SCALE
Jim Samuels, PhD & Jay Klusky, PhD
ISBN: 978-09634011-5-7
LCCN: 2010937464

If you want a better way to understand, predict and change human behavior, this is the book for you.

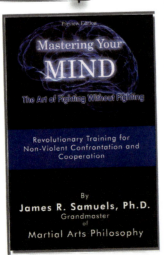

MASTERING YOUR MIND
Jim Samuels, Ph.D.
ISBN-13: 978-1468034899
ISBN-10: 1468034898

If you'd like to expand on your memory, including how to use memory technique to defend yourself from verbal attacks, get this course!

Courses

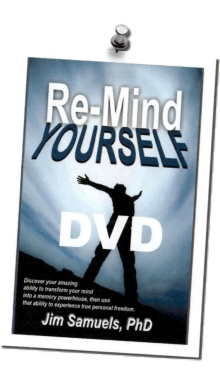

Re-Mind Yourself - DVD

This video course is of a Re-Minding Workshop taught by Dr. Jim Samuels. He explains the Re-Minding technique and gives numerous sessions with a variety of participants to demonstrate its use.

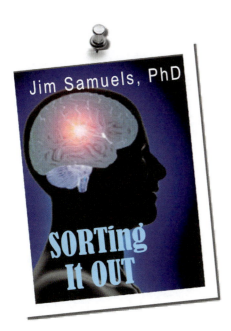

SORTing IT OUT
Jim Samuels, Ph.D.
ISBN-13: 978-1470045463
ISBN-10: 147004546X

This course teaches the technique and benefits of DEEP RE-MINDING™. It's for delving deep into your past to explore chains of events that may have shaped your personality and your future. Set yourself free!

Coming soon

HUMAN GPS & THE WINS FORMULA
Jim Samuels, Ph.D.
ISBN-13: 978-1470045517
ISBN-10: 1470045516
This course shows you a basic function of the human brain and then teaches you the formula for harnessing that function to achieve

PERSONAL FREEDOM!
Jim Samuels, Ph.D.
ISBN-13: 978-1470045487
ISBN-10: 1470045486
Learn what freedom is, how the brain processes choices, and an exercise for expanding your personal freedom beyond anything you thought possible.

Made in the USA
Charleston, SC
21 May 2012